P9-CEU-235

DATE DUE

APR 1 2 2007	OCT ○ 2010
	MAR 0 4 2011

Tugboats

by Lola M. Schaefer

Consultant:
Christopher Hall, President
Hall Associates of Washington, Inc.
Tugboat and Barge Brokerage

Bridgestone Books
an imprint of Capstone Press
Mankato, Minnesota

Bridgestone Books are published by Capstone Press
151 Good Counsel Drive, P.O. Box 669, Mankato, Minnesota 56002
http://www.capstone-press.com

Library of Congress Cataloging-in-Publication Data
Schaefer, Lola M., 1950–
    Tugboats/by Lola M. Schaefer.
    p. cm.—(The transportation library)
    Includes bibliographical references and index.
    Summary: Describes the history, early models, major parts, and jobs of tugboats.
    ISBN 0-7368-0505-2
    1. Tugboats—Juvenile literature. [1. Tugboats] I. Title. II. Series.
VM464.S35 2000
386'.2232—dc21   99-055170
                                                                                    CIP

Editorial Credits

Karen L. Daas, editor; Timothy Halldin, cover designer; Sara A. Sinnard, illustrator;
    Kimberly Danger, photo researcher

Photo Credits

Archive Photos, 14
Bruce Coleman, Inc./S.L. Craig, Jr., 4
Capt. Brendan J. Lally, 12
Gary J. Benson, cover, 18–19, 20
Index Stock Imagery/Sandra Baker, 8–9
James P. Rowan, 16
Ulrike Welsch, 6

1 2 3 4 5 6 05 04 03 02 01 00

Table of Contents

Tugboats

Tugboats are small but powerful boats. They push or pull larger boats. Some tugboats help large ships enter and leave busy harbors. Other tugboats push barges down rivers or across oceans. These tugboats are called push boats.

barge

a long, flat boat used to move cargo; barges do not have engines.

Tugboat Crew

Each tugboat has a trained crew. A captain is in charge of the tugboat and its crew. A mate helps the captain steer the tugboat. An engineer checks the tugboat's engines. Deckhands tie the tugboat's ropes and cables.

wheelhouse

main deck

JONATHAN T.

hull

Parts of a Tugboat

A tugboat has a steel hull with rubber fenders. The hull is the main body of the tugboat. It holds diesel engines. The sleeping quarters and galley usually are on the main deck. The wheelhouse is at the top of the tugboat. The captain steers the boat from the wheelhouse.

galley
a kitchen on a boat

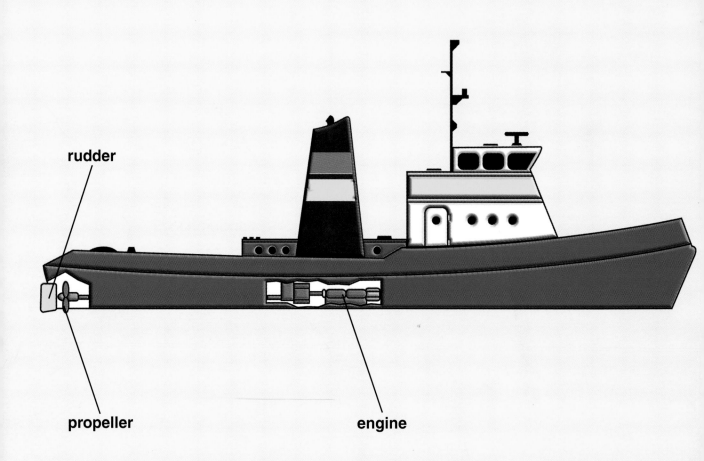

rudder

propeller

engine

How a Tugboat Works

A tugboat pulls a ship with ropes and cables. The tugboat's engines produce power. This power spins propellers. The tugboat moves when the propellers spin. A rudder turns the tugboat.

Steering a Tugboat

A captain steers the tugboat from the wheelhouse. The captain watches other boats, docks, and the weather from the wheelhouse windows. The captain uses a wheel or joystick to steer the tugboat. The captain uses levers to control the tugboat's speed.

joystick

a lever used to control movement

Before the Tugboat

Rowboats helped move ships before tugboats were invented. Rowboats towed large ships in and out of crowded harbors. They also carried cargo between the ships and shore.

paddle wheel

Early Tugboats

In 1802, people in Scotland tested the first tugboat. Steam powered the *Charlotte Dundas*. This tugboat had a wooden hull. Early tugboats had paddle wheels. After 1850, tugboats had propellers instead of paddle wheels.

paddle wheel

a large wheel with boards that turns and moves boats through water

Tugboats Today

Tugboats move barges along coasts, rivers, and oceans. They also move large ships in harbors. Tugboats turn ships around in harbors. Ships are too large to turn themselves around. Tugboats also help ships dock.

Tugboat Facts

- Fire fighters use some tugboats to put out harbor fires. These tugboats pump water from the sea or foam from tanks.

- A tugboat can tow a ship that is 100 times its own weight.

- Tow ropes on a tugboat are more than 6 inches (15 centimeters) thick.

- Three tugboats can turn and dock a large cargo ship in a harbor. The first and second tugboats move the ship to the dock. The third tugboat holds the ship while the crew ties it to the dock.

- Many crews work and live on tugboats for two weeks at a time.

Hands On: Push and Pull

Three tugboats work together to bring a large ship into a harbor. They use ropes to push and pull the ship to the dock. You can learn how tugboats move ships.

What You Need

Wooden craft stick
Two pieces of string
Marker
Rectangular pan half filled with water
A friend

What You Do

1. Tie a piece of string to each end of the craft stick. The stick is like a ship. The strings are like towlines.
2. Mark one end of the stick. This is the the front of your ship.
3. Place your ship in the pan half filled with water.
4. Use the string on the front of your ship to pull the ship toward one end of the pan. Your hand is like the tugboat. This string is like the first towline.
5. Use the string on the back of your ship to turn the ship flat against the side of the pan. This string is like the second towline.
6. Have a friend place a finger against the side of the ship. Your friend's finger is like the third tugboat. This tugboat holds the ship while the crew ties the ship to the dock.

Words to Know

cargo (KAR-goh)—goods that are carried from one place to another

crew (KROO)—a team of people who work together on a ship

diesel (DEE-zuhl)—a heavy fuel that burns to make power; many tugboats run on diesel.

fender (FEN-dur)—a cover that protects the hull against damage

harbor (HAR-bur)—a place where ships unload their cargo

hull (HUHL)—the main body of a tugboat

joystick (JOI-stik)—a lever used to control movement

Read More

Burke, Timothy R. *Tugboats in Action.* Morton Grove, Ill.: Albert Whitman, 1993.

Maass, Robert. *Tugboats.* New York: Holt, 1997.

Maynard, Christopher. *The Usborne Book of Cutaway Boats.* London: Usborne Publishing, 1996.

Internet Sites

Boating Pictures—Tugboats
http://www.boatingpictures.com/powerpix/tugboats/tug.html
Island Tug and Barge Services
http://www.islandtug-barge.com/vessels.html
Tugboat Crossing
http://www.tugboats.com

Index